# ENGLISH
## IRREGULAR VERBS
## COMPLETE

### Learn in Days, Keep Forever

# Fluent English Publishing

Xiao, Ken
Xiao, Urison

English Irregular Verbs Complete: Learn in Days, Keep Forever

ISBN: 978-1-949916-08-9

# CONTENTS

❀

# Chapter 1: Look at the Verbs

You have studied English for years, yet you struggle to tell the difference between regular and irregular verbs. Because of this, you often use the wrong irregular verbs.

The good news is this is very normal.

Ken was once like you, but now he can use the English irregular verbs automatically. Urison published his first book when he was eight. In this book, Ken and Urison will teach you the secret to learn English irregular verbs effortlessly, automatically, and permanently…and they'll teach you how to achieve that in days.

In this book, you will:

- Learn irregular verbs effortlessly
- Learn irregular verbs automatically
- Learn irregular verbs permanently
- Learn irregular verbs quickly

You have studied English for years, yet you still use the incorrect verbs. The reason is simple: The learning methods you've used were ineffective. Change your approach now. 'Learn from an English teacher who has walked in your shoes before and achieved the results you want. Discover what the secret is and follow the secret to learn English irregular verbs quickly and effectively!

# ENGLISH IRREGULAR VERBS COMPLETE

## Chapter 2: Learn the Secret

So, what's the secret? One word: Practice!

Fun fact:
If we read a book, after an hour, we only remember 50%.

Learning English irregular verbs is a lot like swimming. We just need to dive in and begin.

Rather than learning a ton of instructions – which we'll forget after two weeks, we'll learn the irregular verbs by repetition that instills them into our subconscious mind.

Read the irregular verbs in this book aloud, over and over. If you have the audio version, listen to and repeat the audio many times. Once we get the information into our subconscious mind, our use of the irregular verbs will become automatic.

# ENGLISH IRREGULAR VERBS COMPLETE

# Chapter 3: Take the Steps

How do we get the irregular verbs into our subconscious mind?

**Practice!**

Do you drive? Do you take the bus? The train? Do you walk? Do you work out? Do you cook? Do you wait in line for anything? Do you have moments in your days when your body is busy but your mind is free?

These moments are great for repeating irregular verbs to ingrain them in our subconscious mind.

Even if a moment is just 60 seconds, put on our headphones, listen and repeat.

# ENGLISH IRREGULAR VERBS COMPLETE

# Chapter 4: Learn the Patterns

In this book, you'll learn a complete list of English irregular verbs. First, let's learn the irregular verbs that have specific conjugation patterns.

1. In the following table, change all verbs from -ay to -aid:

| Verb | Past Tense | Past Participle |
|------|------------|-----------------|
| lay | laid | laid |
| mislay | mislaid | mislaid |
| pay | paid | paid |
| say | said | said |

## 2. In the following table, change -eep to -ept:

| Verb | Past Tense | Past Participle |
|------|------------|-----------------|
| creep | crept | crept |
| keep | kept | kept |
| sleep | slept | slept |
| sweep | swept | swept |
| weep | wept | wept |

3. In the following table, change -ang and -ing to -ung:

| Verb | Past Tense | Past Participle |
|---|---|---|
| cling | clung | clung |
| fling | flung | flung |
| hang | hung | hung |
| sling | slung | slung |
| spring | sprung | sprung |
| sting | stung | stung |
| string | strung | strung |
| swing | swung | swung |
| wring | wrung | wrung |

4. In the following table, change -ell to -old:

| Verb | Past Tense | Past Participle |
|------|-----------|-----------------|
| sell | sold | sold |
| tell | told | told |

5. In the following table, change -d to -t:

| Verb | Past Tense | Past Participle |
| --- | --- | --- |
| bend | bent | bent |
| build | built | built |
| lend | lent | lent |
| send | sent | sent |
| spend | spent | spent |

6. In the following table, remove the second vowel:

| Verb | Past Tense | Past Participle |
| --- | --- | --- |
| bleed | bled | bled |
| breed | bred | bred |
| feed | fed | fed |
| flee | fled | fled |
| lead | led | led |
| meet | met | met |
| plead | pled | pled |
| shoot | shot | shot |
| speed | sped | sped |

7. In the following table, for the past, replace the stressed vowels with o, and for the past participle, add n at the end:

| Verb | Past Tense | Past Participle |
|------|------------|-----------------|
| arise | arose | arisen |
| awake | awoke | awoken |
| break | broke | broken |
| drive | drove | driven |
| forget | forgot | forgotten |
| forgive | forgave | forgiven |
| freeze | froze | frozen |
| get | got | gotten |
| ride | rode | ridden |
| rise | rose | risen |
| speak | spoke | spoken |
| steal | stole | stolen |
| strive | strove | striven |
| tread | trod | trodden |
| wake | woke | woken |
| weave | wove | woven |
| write | wrote | written |

8. In the following table, for the past, replace -ear with -ore, and for the past participle, replace it with -orn or -orne.

| Verb | Past Tense | Past Participle |
|------|-----------|-----------------|
| bear | bore | borne |
| swear | swore | sworn |
| wear | wore | worn |

9. In the following table, all irregular verbs in the past and the past participle end in aught:

| Verb | Past Tense | Past Participle |
|------|-----------|-----------------|
| catch | caught | caught |
| teach | taught | taught |

10. In the following table, all irregular verbs in the past and the past participle end in ought:

| Verb | Past Tense | Past Participle |
|---|---|---|
| bring | brought | brought |
| buy | bought | bought |
| fight | fought | fought |
| seek | sought | sought |
| think | thought | thought |

11. In the following table, change all verbs that end in -l to -lt.

| Verb | Past Tense | Past Participle |
|------|-----------|-----------------|
| deal | dealt | dealt |
| dwell | dwelt | dwelt |
| feel | felt | felt |
| kneel | knelt | knelt |

12. In the following table, all irregular verbs in all forms stay the same:

| Verb | Past Tense | Past Participle |
| --- | --- | --- |
| beat | beat | beat |
| bet | bet | bet |
| bid | bid | bid |
| broadcast | broadcast | broadcast |
| burst | burst | burst |
| cast | cast | cast |
| cost | cost | cost |
| cut | cut | cut |
| fit | fit | fit |
| forecast | forecast | forecast |
| hit | hit | hit |
| hurt | hurt | hurt |
| input | input | input |
| let | let | let |
| put | put | put |
| quit | quit | quit |
| read | read | read |
| rid | rid | rid |
| set | set | set |
| shed | shed | shed |
| shut | shut | shut |
| slingshot | slingshot | slingshot |
| slit | slit | slit |
| spit | spit | spit |
| split | split | split |
| spread | spread | spread |
| thrust | thrust | thrust |
| upset | upset | upset |

KEN XIAO & URISON XIAO

# ENGLISH IRREGULAR VERBS COMPLETE

# Chapter 5: Use the Common Ones

## Fun fact:

The most frequently used English irregular verb is *be*, which can also appear as am, is, are, was, were, and been. The most frequently used English regular verb is *ask*.

The verbs in the following table are used frequently. They're called common irregular verbs. These common irregular verbs are the most useful English irregular verbs.

| Verb | Past Tense | Past Participle |
|------|-----------|-----------------|
| arise | arose | arisen |
| awake | awoke | awoken |
| be | was/were | been |
| bear | bore | borne |
| beat | beat | beat |
| become | became | become |
| begin | began | begun |
| bend | bent | bent |
| bet | bet | bet |
| bid | bid | bid |
| bind | bound | bound |
| bite | bit | bitten |
| bleed | bled | bled |
| blow | blew | blown |
| break | broke | broken |
| breed | bred | bred |
| bring | brought | brought |
| broadcast | broadcast | broadcast |
| build | built | built |
| burst | burst | burst |
| buy | bought | bought |

| | | |
|---|---|---|
| cast | cast | cast |
| catch | caught | caught |
| choose | chose | chosen |
| cling | clung | clung |
| come | came | come |
| cost | cost | cost |
| creep | crept | crept |
| cut | cut | cut |
| deal | dealt | dealt |
| dig | dug | dug |
| dive | dove | dived |
| do | did | done |
| draw | drew | drawn |
| drink | drank | drunk |
| drive | drove | driven |
| dwell | dwelt | dwelt |
| eat | ate | eaten |
| fall | fell | fallen |
| feed | fed | fed |
| feel | felt | felt |
| fight | fought | fought |
| find | found | found |
| fit | fit | fit |
| flee | fled | fled |
| fling | flung | flung |
| fly | flew | flown |
| forbid | forbade | forbidden |
| forecast | forecast | forecast |
| forget | forgot | forgotten |
| forgive | forgave | forgiven |
| forsake | forsook | forsaken |
| freeze | froze | frozen |
| get | got | gotten |
| give | gave | given |
| go | went | gone |
| grind | ground | ground |

| | | |
|---|---|---|
| grow | grew | grown |
| hang | hung | hung |
| have | had | had |
| hear | heard | heard |
| heave | heaved | hove |
| hew | hewed | hewn |
| hide | hid | hidden |
| hit | hit | hit |
| hold | held | held |
| hurt | hurt | hurt |
| input | input | input |
| keep | kept | kept |
| kneel | knelt | knelt |
| know | knew | known |
| lay | laid | laid |
| lead | led | led |
| leap | leapt | leapt |
| leave | left | left |
| lend | lent | lent |
| let | let | let |
| lie | lay | lain |
| light | lit | lit |
| lose | lost | lost |
| make | made | made |
| mean | meant | meant |
| meet | met | met |
| mow | mowed | mown |
| overcome | overcame | overcome |
| pay | paid | paid |
| plead | pled | pled |
| prove | proved | proven |
| put | put | put |
| quit | quit | quit |
| read | read | read |
| rid | rid | rid |
| ride | rode | ridden |

| | | |
|---|---|---|
| ring | rang | rung |
| rise | rose | risen |
| run | ran | run |
| saw | sawed | sawn |
| say | said | said |
| see | saw | seen |
| seek | sought | sought |
| sell | sold | sold |
| send | sent | sent |
| set | set | set |
| sew | sewed | sewn |
| shake | shook | shaken |
| shear | sheared | shorn |
| shed | shed | shed |
| shine | shone | shone |
| shoot | shot | shot |
| show | showed | shown |
| shrink | shrank | shrunk |
| shut | shut | shut |
| sing | sang | sung |
| sink | sank | sunk |
| sit | sat | sat |
| slay | slew | slain |
| sleep | slept | slept |
| slide | slid | slid |
| sling | slung | slung |
| slit | slit | slit |
| sow | sowed | sown |
| speak | spoke | spoken |
| speed | sped | sped |
| spend | spent | spent |
| spin | spun | spun |
| spit | spit | spit |
| split | split | split |
| spread | spread | spread |
| spring | sprung | sprung |

| | | |
|---|---|---|
| stand | stood | stood |
| steal | stole | stolen |
| stick | stuck | stuck |
| sting | stung | stung |
| stink | stank | stunk |
| stride | strode | stridden |
| strike | struck | struck |
| string | strung | strung |
| strive | strove | striven |
| swear | swore | sworn |
| sweep | swept | swept |
| swell | swelled | swollen |
| swim | swam | swum |
| swing | swung | swung |
| take | took | taken |
| teach | taught | taught |
| tear | tore | torn |
| tell | told | told |
| think | thought | thought |
| thrive | throve | thriven |
| throw | threw | thrown |
| thrust | thrust | thrust |
| tread | trod | trodden |
| understand | understood | understood |
| upset | upset | upset |
| wake | woke | woken |
| wear | wore | worn |
| weave | wove | woven |
| weep | wept | wept |
| win | won | won |
| wind | wound | wound |
| withdraw | withdrew | withdrawn |
| withstand | withstood | withstood |
| wring | wrung | wrung |
| write | wrote | written |

# ENGLISH IRREGULAR VERBS COMPLETE

# Chapter 6: Know the Complete List

The following is the complete list of English irregular verbs.

| Verb | Past Tense | Past Participle |
|------|-----------|-----------------|
| abide | abode | abode |
| arise | arose | arisen |
| be | was/were | been |
| bear | bore | borne |
| beat | beat | beat |
| become | became | become |
| bedrive | bedrove | bedriven |
| befall | befell | befallen |
| befly | beflew | beflown |
| beget | begot | begotten |
| begin | began | begun |
| begive | begave | begiven |
| behold | beheld | beheld |
| beknow | beknew | beknown |
| belive | belove | beliven |
| bend | bent | bent |
| bequeath | bequoth | bequethen |
| besee | besaw | beseen |
| beseech | besought | besought |
| beshake | beshook | beshaken |

| | | |
|---|---|---|
| bespeak | bespoke | bespoken |
| besteal | bestole | bestolen |
| bestrew | bestrewed | bestrewn |
| bet | bet | bet |
| betake | betook | betaken |
| bethrow | bethrew | bethrown |
| bid | bid | bid |
| bide | bode | bidden |
| bind | bound | bound |
| bite | bit | bitten |
| bleed | bled | bled |
| blow | blew | blown |
| break | broke | broken |
| break-up | broke-up | Broken-up |
| breed | bred | bred |
| bring | brought | brought |
| broadcast | broadcast | broadcast |
| browbeat | browbeat | browbeaten |
| build | built | built |
| burst | burst | burst |
| buy | bought | bought |
| caretake | caretook | caretaken |
| cast | cast | cast |
| catch | caught | caught |
| chide | chid | chid |

| | | |
|---|---|---|
| choose | chose | chosen |
| cling | clung | clung |
| co-write | co-wrote | co-written |
| come | came | come |
| copywrite | copywrote | copywritten |
| counterdraw | counterdrew | counterdrawn |
| countersink | countersank | countersunk |
| cost | cost | cost |
| cowrite | cowrote | cowritten |
| creep | crept | crept |
| crossbite | crossbit | crossbitten |
| cut | cut | cut |
| deal | dealt | dealt |
| deep-freeze | deep-froze | deep-frozen |
| dig | dug | dug |
| disprove | disproved | disproven |
| dive | dove | dived |
| do | did | done |
| downbear | downbore | downborne |
| downfall | downfell | downfallen |
| draw | drew | drawn |
| drink | drank | drunk |
| drive | drove | driven |
| eat | ate | eaten |
| enfreeze | enfroze | enfrozen |

| | | |
|---|---|---|
| enwrite | enwrote | enwritten |
| fall | fell | fallen |
| feed | fed | fed |
| feel | felt | felt |
| fight | fought | fought |
| find | found | found |
| fistfight | fistfought | fistfought |
| fit | fit | fit |
| flee | fled | fled |
| fling | flung | flung |
| fly | flew | flown |
| forbear | forbore | forborne |
| forbeat | forbeat | forbeaten |
| forbid | forbade | forbidden |
| forbreak | forbroke | forbroken |
| forburst | forburst | forburst |
| fordo | fordid | fordone |
| fordrive | fordrove | fordriven |
| forebear | forebore | foreborne |
| forecast | forecast | forecast |
| forego | forewent | foregone |
| foreknow | foreknew | foreknown |
| forerun | foreran | forerun |
| foresee | foresaw | foreseen |
| foreshow | foreshowed | foreshown |

| | | |
|---|---|---|
| forespeak | forespoke | forespoken |
| foreswear | foreswore | foresworn |
| foretake | foretook | foretaken |
| forget | forgot | forgotten |
| forgive | forgave | forgiven |
| forgo | forwent | forgone |
| forhold | forheld | forheld |
| forsake | forsook | forsaken |
| forswear | forswore | forsworn |
| forthcome | forthcame | forthcome |
| forthgo | forthwent | forthgone |
| freefall | freefell | freefallen |
| freeride | freerode | freeridden |
| freerun | freeran | freerun |
| freeze | froze | frozen |
| frostbite | frostbit | frostbitten |
| fulldo | fulldid | fulldone |
| get | got | got or gotten |
| give | gave | given |
| go | went | gone |
| grave | graved | graven |
| grind | ground | ground |
| grow | grew | grown |
| handwrite | handwrote | handwritten |
| hang | hung | hung |

| | | |
|---|---|---|
| have | had | had |
| hear | heard | heard |
| heatsink | Heatsank | heatsunk |
| heave | heaved | hove |
| hew | hewed | hewn |
| hide | hid | hidden |
| hit | hit | hit |
| hold | held | held |
| housebreak | housebroke | housebroken |
| hurt | hurt | hurt |
| inbear | inbore | inborne |
| inbeat | inbeat | inbeaten |
| inbreak | inbroke | inbroken |
| ingrow | ingrew | ingrown |
| intergrow | intergrew | intergrown |
| interknow | interknew | interknown |
| interweave | interwove | interwoven |
| inwrite | inwrote | inwritten |
| jailbreak | jailbroke | jailbroken |
| jigsaw | jigsawed | jigsawn |
| joyride | joyrode | joyridden |
| keep | kept | kept |
| kneel | knelt | knelt |
| know | knew | known |
| lade | laded | laden |

| | | |
|---|---|---|
| lay | laid | laid |
| lead | led | led |
| leap | leapt | leapt |
| leave | left | left |
| lend | lent | lent |
| let | let | let |
| lie | lay | lain |
| light | lit | lit |
| lose | lost | lost |
| make | made | made |
| mean | meant | meant |
| meet | met | met |
| mis-hit | mis-hit | mis-hit |
| misbid | misbid | misbid |
| mischoose | mischose | mischosen |
| misdo | misdid | misdone |
| misfall | misfell | misfallen |
| misgive | misgave | misgiven |
| misgo | miswent | misgone |
| mishold | misheld | misheld |
| misspeak | misspoke | misspoken |
| mistake | mistook | mistaken |
| misthrow | misthrew | misthrown |
| miswrite | miswrote | miswritten |
| offhold | offheld | offheld |

| | | |
|---|---|---|
| offtake | offtook | offtaken |
| onfall | onfell | onfallen |
| outbreak | outbroke | outbroken |
| outburst | outburst | outburst |
| outcreep | outcrept | outcrept |
| outdo | outdid | outdone |
| outdraw | outdrew | outdrawn |
| outdrive | outdrove | outdriven |
| outeat | outate | outeaten |
| outfall | outfell | outfallen |
| outfly | outflew | outflown |
| outgive | outgave | outgiven |
| outgo | outwent | outgone |
| outgrow | outgrew | outgrown |
| outhold | outheld | outheld |
| outride | outrode | outridden |
| outrun | outran | outrun |
| outsee | outsaw | outseen |
| outsing | outsang | outsung |
| outspeak | outspoke | outspoken |
| outspring | outsprang | outsprung |
| outswim | outswam | outswum |
| outtake | outtook | outtaken |
| outthrow | outthrew | outthrown |
| outwrite | outwrote | outwritten |

| | | |
|---|---|---|
| overbear | overbore | overborne |
| overbeat | overbeat | overbeaten |
| overblow | overblew | overblown |
| overbreak | overbroke | overbroken |
| overcome | overcame | overcome |
| overdo | overdid | overdone |
| overdraw | overdrew | overdrawn |
| overdrink | overdrank | overdrunk |
| overdrive | overdrove | overdriven |
| overeat | overate | overeaten |
| overfly | overflew | overflown |
| overgo | overwent | overgone |
| overgrow | overgrew | overgrown |
| overhold | overheld | overheld |
| overlade | overladed | overladen |
| overlie | overlay | overlain |
| override | overrode | overridden |
| overrun | overran | overrun |
| oversee | oversaw | overseen |
| overtake | overtook | overtaken |
| overthrow | overthrew | overthrown |
| overtread | overtrod | overtrodden |
| overwrite | overwrote | overwritten |
| partake | partook | partaken |
| pay | paid | paid |

| | | |
|---|---|---|
| piledrive | piledrove | piledriven |
| plead | pled | pled |
| pratfall | pratfell | pratfallen |
| prepay | prepaid | prepaid |
| preshow | preshowed | preshown |
| preshrink | preshrank | preshrunk |
| prewrite | prewrote | prewritten |
| prove | proved | proven |
| put | put | put |
| quick-freeze | quick-froze | quick-frozen |
| quit | quit | quit |
| re-run | re-ran | re-run |
| re-sew | re-sewed | re-sewn |
| read | read | read |
| reawake | reawoke | reawoken |
| rebear | rebore | reborne |
| rebecome | rebecame | rebecome |
| rebegin | rebegan | rebegun |
| rebreak | rebroke | rebroken |
| redo | redid | redone |
| redraw | redrew | redrawn |
| refreeze | refroze | refrozen |
| regrow | regrew | regrown |
| rerun | reran | rerun |
| resaw | resawed | resawn |

| | | |
|---|---|---|
| resew | resewed | resewn |
| restrike | restruck | restruck |
| retake | retook | retaken |
| rethrow | rethrew | rethrown |
| rewake | rewoke | rewoken |
| reweave | rewove | rewoven |
| rewrite | rewrote | rewritten |
| rid | rid | rid |
| ride | rode | ridden |
| ring | rang | rung |
| rise | rose | risen |
| rive | rived | riven |
| roadshow | roadshowed | roadshown |
| run | ran | run |
| saw | sawed | sawn |
| say | said | said |
| see | saw | seen |
| seek | sought | sought |
| sell | sold | sold |
| send | sent | sent |
| set | set | set |
| shake | shook | shaken |
| shall | should | - |
| shear | sheared | shorn |
| shed | shed | shed |

| | | |
|---|---|---|
| shine | shone | shone |
| shoe | shod | shod |
| shoot | shot | shot |
| show | showed | shown |
| shrink | shrank | shrunk |
| shrive | shrove | shriven |
| shut | shut | shut |
| sightsee | sightsaw | sightseen |
| sing | sang | sung |
| sink | sank | sunk |
| sit | sat | sat |
| slay | slew | slain |
| sleep | slept | slept |
| slide | slid | slid |
| sling | Slung | slung |
| slingshot | slingshot | slingshot |
| slit | slit | slit |
| sow | sowed | sown |
| speak | spoke | spoken |
| speed | sped | sped |
| spend | spent | spent |
| spin | spun | spun |
| spit | spit | spit |
| spread | spread | spread |
| spring | sprang | sprung |

| | | |
|---|---|---|
| stand | stood | stood |
| steal | stole | stolen |
| sting | stung | stung |
| stink | stank | stunk |
| strew | strewed | strewn |
| stride | strode | stridden |
| strike | struck | struck |
| string | strung | strung |
| strive | strove | striven |
| swear | swore | sworn |
| sweep | swept | swept |
| swell | swelled | swollen |
| swim | swam | swum |
| swing | swang | swung |
| take | took | taken |
| teach | taught | taught |
| tear | tore | torn |
| tell | told | told |
| test-drive | test-drove | test-driven |
| test-fly | test-flew | test-flown |
| think | thought | thought |
| thrive | throve | thriven |
| throw | threw | thrown |
| thrust | thrust | thrust |
| tread | trod | trodden |

| | | |
|---|---|---|
| typewrite | typewrote | typewritten |
| un-break | un-broke | un-broken |
| unbecome | unbecame | unbecome |
| unbid | unbid | unbid |
| unbind | unbound | unbound |
| unbreak | unbroke | unbroken |
| unchoose | unchose | unchosen |
| undercome | undercame | undercome |
| underdo | underdid | underdone |
| understand | understood | understood |
| unhide | unhid | unhidden |
| unknow | unknew | unknown |
| unlade | unladed | unladen |
| unweave | unwove | unwoven |
| unwrite | unwrote | unwritten |
| upbreak | upbroke | upbroken |
| updraw | updrew | updrawn |
| upgrow | upgrew | upgrown |
| uphold | upheld | upheld |
| upleap | upleapt | upleapt |
| uprun | upran | uprun |
| upset | upset | upset |
| upspeak | upspoke | upspoken |
| upspring | upsprang | upsprung |
| upswell | upswelled | upswollen |

| | | |
|---|---|---|
| uptear | uptore | uptorn |
| upthrow | upthrew | upthrown |
| wake | woke | woken |
| wardrive | wardrove | wardriven |
| wear | wore | worn |
| weave | wove | woven |
| weep | wept | wept |
| will | would | - |
| win | won | won |
| wind | wound | wound |
| wind-break | wind-broke | wind-broken |
| wiredraw | wiredrew | wiredrawn |
| withbear | withbore | withborne |
| withdraw | withdrew | withdrawn |
| withstand | withstood | withstood |
| wring | wrung | wrung |
| write | wrote | written |

# ENGLISH IRREGULAR VERBS COMPLETE

# Chapter 7: To Be, or Not To Be

The following is a list of English irregular verbs from Old English to Middle English. These irregular verbs are not being used today, but to learn, or not to learn, that is the question.

| Verb | Past Tense | Past Participle |
|------|-----------|-----------------|
| abear | abore | aborne |
| abite | abit | abitten |
| acknow | acknew | acknown |
| adraw | adrew | adrawn |
| aftersee | aftersaw | afterseen |
| aknow | aknew | aknown |
| arize | aroze | arizen |
| atgo | atwent | atgone |
| atride | atrode | atridden |
| atrin | atran | atrun |
| atrine | atrone | atrinnen |
| atsake | atsook | atsaken |
| atshake | atshook | atshaken |
| atsit | atsat | atsat |
| bedelve | bedolve | bedolven |
| bedo | bedid | bedone |
| bedraw | bedrew | bedrawn |
| bedrink | bedrank | bedrunk |

| | | |
|---|---|---|
| bedrite | bedrote | bedritten |
| bego | bewent | begone |
| behew | behewed | behewn |
| belawgive | belawgave | belawgiven |
| belimp | belamp | belump |
| benim | benam | benomen |
| beride | berode | beridden |
| beshear | beshore | beshorn |
| besing | besang | besung |
| besit | besat | besitten |
| bespit | bespat | bespit |
| bestride | bestrode | bestrode |
| beswike | beswoke | beswicken |
| betread | betrod | betrodden |
| bewrite | bewrote | bewritten |
| clepe | clept | clept |
| countersing | countersang | countersung |
| disbecome | disbecame | disbecome |
| downcome | downcame | downcome |
| downdraw | downdrew | downdrawn |
| downtrod | downtrod | downtrodden |
| drite | drate | dritten |
| enblow | enblew | enblown |
| entertake | entertook | entertaken |
| farsee | farsaw | farseen |

| | | |
|---|---|---|
| farspeak | farspoke | farspoken |
| finedraw | finedrew | finedrawn |
| fistfight | fistfought | fistfought |
| flyblow | flyblew | flyblown |
| forbite | forbit | forbitten |
| forcleave | forclove | forcloven |
| forebite | forebit | forebitten |
| forechoose | forechose | forechosen |
| foredo | foredid | foredone |
| foredraw | foredrew | foredrawn |
| forehew | forehewed | forehewn |
| forehold | foreheld | foreheld |
| forelie | forelay | forelain |
| foreshew | foreshewed | foreshewn |
| forfight | forfought | forfought |
| forgrow | forgrew | forgrown |
| forlie | forlay | forlain |
| fornim | fornam | fornum |
| forsee | forsaw | forseen |
| forshake | forshook | forshaken |
| forshrink | forshrank | forshrunk |
| forsing | forsang | forsung |
| forsling | forslung | forslung |
| forsmite | forsmote | forsmitten |
| forspeak | forspoke | forspoken |

| | | |
|---|---|---|
| forsteal | forstole | forstolen |
| forswing | forswang | forswung |
| forswink | forswank | forswunk |
| fortake | fortook | fortaken |
| fortear | fortore | fortorn |
| forthbear | forthbore | forthborn |
| forthdraw | forthdrew | forthdrawn |
| forthnim | forthnam | forthnum |
| forthrow | forthrew | forthrown |
| forthshow | forthshowed | forthshown |
| forthspeak | forthspoke | forthspoken |
| fortread | fortrod | fortrodden |
| forwear | forwore | forworn |
| fullcome | fullcame | fullcome |
| gainstrive | gainstrove | gainstriven |
| inblow | inblew | inblown |
| infall | infell | infallen |
| inhold | inheld | inheld |
| insee | insaw | inseen |
| instrew | instrewed | instrewn |
| intercome | intercame | intercome |
| inweave | inwove | inwoven |
| manswear | manswore | mansworn |
| misbear | misbore | misborne |
| misbeat | misbeat | misbeaten |

| | | |
|---|---|---|
| misbefall | misbefell | misbefallen |
| miscleave | misclove | miscloven |
| miscome | miscame | miscome |
| misget | misgot | misgotten |
| misgrow | misgrew | misgrown |
| misknow | misknew | misknown |
| mislie | mislay | mislain |
| missee | missaw | misseen |
| misswear | misswore | missworn |
| miswear | miswore | misworn |
| nim | nam | nomen |
| noseride | noserode | noseridden |
| offsmite | offsmote | offsmitten |
| onhold | onheld | onheld |
| ontake | ontook | ontaken |
| outbear | outbore | outborne |
| outnim | outnam | outnomen |
| outring | outrang | outrung |
| outrive | outrove | outriven |
| outshow | outshowed | outshown |
| outstink | outstank | outstunk |
| outstrike | outstruck | outstruck |
| outswear | outswore | outsworn |
| outswell | outswelled | outswollen |
| overfall | overfell | overfallen |

| | | |
|---|---|---|
| overget | overgot | overgotten |
| overgive | overgave | overgiven |
| overshake | overshook | overshaken |
| oversow | oversowed | oversown |
| overspeak | overspoke | overspoken |
| overspring | oversprang | oversprung |
| overstraw | overstrawed | overstrawn |
| overstrew | overstrewed | overstrewn |
| overstrow | overstrowed | overstrown |
| overwear | overwore | overworn |
| prerun | preran | prerun |
| presew | presewed | presewn |
| quartersaw | quartersawed | quartersawn |
| rechoose | rechose | rechosen |
| refall | refell | refallen |
| refly | reflew | reflown |
| regive | regave | regiven |
| rehew | rehewed | rehewn |
| rehide | rehid | rehidden |
| resee | resaw | reseen |
| reshake | reshook | reshaken |
| resow | resowed | resown |
| respeak | respoke | respoken |
| restrive | restrove | restriven |
| reswear | reswore | resworn |

| | | |
|---|---|---|
| retear | retore | retorn |
| rin | ran | run |
| rough-hew | rough-hewed | rough-hewn |
| roughhew | roughhewed | roughhewn |
| showrun | showran | showrun |
| smite | smote | smitten |
| speedrun | speedran | speedrun |
| strow | strowed | strown |
| superlie | superlay | superlain |
| talebear | talebore | taleborne |
| thanksgive | thanksgave | thanksgiven |
| thoroughgo | thoroughwent | thoroughgone |
| thunderstrike | thunderstruck | thunderstruck |
| tobeat | tobeat | tobeaten |
| tobreak | tobroke | tobroken |
| toburst | toburst | toburst |
| tocleave | toclove | tocloven |
| todraw | todrew | todrawn |
| todrive | todrove | todriven |
| togo | towent | togone |
| tohew | tohewed | tohewn |
| toshake | toshook | toshaken |
| toshear | toshore | toshorn |
| totear | totore | totorn |
| totread | totrod | totrodden |

| | | |
|---|---|---|
| unbear | unbore | unborne |
| underbear | underbore | underborne |
| undercreep | undercrept | undercrept |
| unsee | unsaw | unseen |
| unsew | unsewed | unsewn |
| unspeak | unspoke | unspoken |
| unswear | unswore | unsworn |
| unswell | unswelled | unswollen |
| upbear | upbore | upborne |
| upblow | upblew | upblown |
| upcome | upcame | upcome |
| upgive | upgave | upgiven |
| uprise | uprose | uprisen |

KEN XIAO & URISON XIAO

# ENGLISH IRREGULAR VERBS COMPLETE

# Chapter 8: The Secret to Learn the Irregular Verbs

## Fun fact:
If we read a book, after three days, we only remember 25%.

You'll recall that learning irregular verbs is a lot like learning how to swim. By going through this book once, you jumped into the pool, but going through this book only once or twice is far from enough. Instead, you'll have the most learning success if you go continually repeat the irregular verbs in this book until they become ingrained knowledge.

# ENGLISH IRREGULAR VERBS COMPLETE

# About the Authors

## KEN XIAO

KEN is a role model of English learners. He successfully learned to speak English like a native speaker in six months using a formula he'd discovered. He had been an interpreter with the United States Department of Defense. He is now an English teacher, school principal, and author.

## URISON XIAO

URISON published his first book when he was eight years old. He likes to write and writes every day. While his first book is a comic, the book he's currently writing is a novel.

# ENGLISH IRREGULAR VERBS COMPLETE

# Other books by Ken Xiao and Urison Xiao

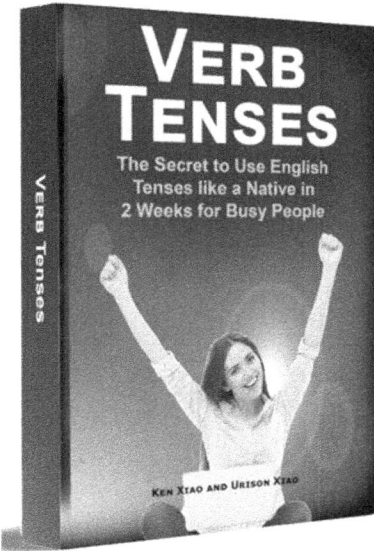

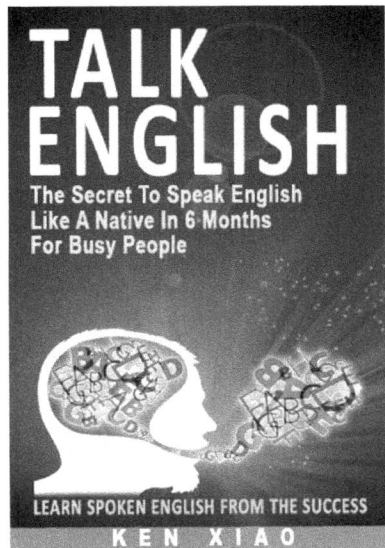

www.ingramcontent.com/pod-product-compliance
Lightning Source LLC
Chambersburg PA
CBHW060537030426
42337CB00021B/4316